come see about me, marvin

Made in Michigan Writers Series

GENERAL EDITORS
Michael Delp, Interlochen Center for the Arts
M. L. Liebler, Wayne State University

A complete listing of the books in this series can be found online at wsupress.wayne.edu

come see about me, marvin

poems by
brian g. gilmore

Wayne State
University Press
Detroit

for m.l. & marvin

ISBN 978-0-8143-4722-5 (paperback)
ISBN 978-0-8143-4723-2 (e-book)

Library of Congress Control Number: 2019944113

Publication of this book was made possible by a generous gift from The Meijer Foundation. This work is supported in part by an award from the Michigan Council for Arts and Cultural Affairs.

Wayne State University Press
Leonard N. Simons Building
4809 Woodward Avenue
Detroit, Michigan 48201–1309

Visit us online at wsupress.wayne.edu

Contents

3. no ordinary pain

4. let your love come shining through

love that will shelter you

distant lover #1
(my michigan bed remix—for ellen g)

dear lover. where you
once slept there are
books now. langston
hughes's *the weary blues*
& one about the kent
state shootings, 1970.
i don't read the books.
they are there to fill
the space. i hold hands
w/the books under the
covers, lover, think of them
as i doze off & dream of
you so far away. i imagine you
there beside me
reading in bed like
you did once; i
remember you saying
you would not be gone
long. it has been awhile,
lover. there are a lot
of books there &
looks like many
more to come as the
space seems to get
larger & larger
the longer you are
gone though now
i have grown accustomed
to sleeping w/books.

last night, i began
to read the book

about how the
president once had
some students
murdered at kent
state university &
no one went to jail.
i met a woman once
who was a roommate
of one of the victims.
her room at kent
state suddenly
empty & quiet like
my room is each
night. she had nothing
to fill up the space. her
roommate dying every day
again, telling her she
would be back soon, she
was going to an anti-war
rally.

i have books &
your promise, lover, that
you will return, lay next
to me & read some-
thing or do nothing
at all but be here, alive
& in the big space you
created when you
departed. even
as i try to pretend
i can replace you
w/some books.

mardi gras in east lansing

somehow someway we have to hold onto ourselves
up here. black ice roads. quiet soulless winter.

vitamin d depletion. lucille clifton, something
has chosen to kill me apparently. i'm an idiot;

i am not from buffalo. i seek out the saints. don
a mask, make jambalaya; blast longhair, nevilles

toussaint; make floats out of shoeboxes. recall
return, like jews, poland, palestine, america, u.k.

custom sustains. ritual as rejuvenation. these frozen
streets near my home now named for the conquered are

no help either: cherokee. okemos. chippewa. that is why
i got to play "indian red" in my car every day loud. &

then there are all of those paczkis: sweet, endorphinal
rushes emptier than sinners stripping naked on canal

for strangers. i need the zulu kings. the krewes? or its
equal: the feeling fess gives floating along singing "hey girl."

trouble lurks too. i go blind during lent. vision is
kaleidoscope. a man parties hard on mardi gras to try

to carry on & then becomes ray charles? i am thinking
marie laveau. what did i do or not do? a doctor sees i am

black, says on cue: diabetes. though my blood sugar is
almost always like a soldier seeking stripes. this is karmic

payback for insulting an ancestor. ishmael reed would
probably have said: hire a band. djembe drummers. cornet

carriers. summon up some souls. your eye irritated by
ignorance. like a schoolteacher who sees the exceptional

slacking. from here on out, off w/the mask. dance in
the streets like martha & the vandellas. do not wait until it

is time for mischief to protect your body & soul. be buddy
bolden every day all day. mash this marsh in your mind. it's

your warm blanket night & day. like a hot tea i.v., your
people blowing some blessed summer wind into your woe.

detroit airport, december 2009 (a sermon)

when i came here for the very
first time. (when he came here)
i say when i came here for the
very first time, i thought of
the death of otis redding.
it was snowing. (snowing)
wind was whipping through
my body like needles into
cloth. (cloth). i say when i
came here. (when
he came here). otis redding
don' come to mind. he went
down in some plane that
james brown told him not
to board. & you know if
james brown say don't
do it, that means don't
do it. but angels must have
been on my plane. (angels).
because it was snowing. &
the wind was blowing on the
tarmac (yes) in romulus,
michigan. (yes, romulus).
like you know they call
it the detroit airport but it
is really in a city
so far away you can't
even see the giant gm
building down in detroit.
romulus, that got something
to do w/rome i heard, &
that is how far away you feel
when you are at the detroit
airport. like you are in rome.

but the reason why i
say angels was on the
plane is because i was
warm & calm as if my
wife had a baby & the
baby was in my arms just
fine. & even if you don't
believe in angels, even if you
don't believe in anything you
still got to understand that
otis redding was on my mind.
he got on some small little
plane one day in 1967
w/almost all the members of the
bar-kays band & the plane
crashed. (crashed). not far from here in
lake morona. wisconsin
foggy night. they all died
except one of them.

but this wasn't no foggy
night. this was snow
& wind that felt like
glass pricking my face.
but i brushed it all aside.
(brushed it). like it was a
bad dream that never
started. & i still don't
know why i had my mind
on otis. because really i
wasn't thinking of otis
redding or angels. i was
thinking of my father. how
he would be laughing
right about now
hearing about me on
some small plane.

he knows i was afraid
of bicycles at first &
rollercoasters even if
he held my hand all
the way. & here i was

on a plane that
took off from some
town called romulus
& did I tell you i was
doing crossword
puzzles? my mother
always does crossword
puzzles because it is
like meditation. so i
did crossword puzzles
as the plane took off
headed to lansing, michigan
(yes sir). to teach law. & it
is as cold as a walk-in freezer
but i feel warm. warm
as hot rolls out the oven.

i am not me at all. i just
walk out onto that tarmac
(yes sir). & board
the plane like i am
a famous rhythm &
blues singer headed
for his next show.
(yes). like otis. (otis).
& i am going to make
it to my show. i got
a few things to say.
i used to tremble when
i spoke in front of people
but after that ride on that

small plane i speak good now.
no quiver in my voice.
i just think of the
snow & ice-cold wind
smacking my face that night.
how i strutted w/my
bags. my heart didn't
pound. my legs didn't
shake like tambourines.
nothing got to me suddenly.
i was as calm as that voice
on those shipping reports
on the radio in england.
that soft, precise sound.
the soothing balm of
human vocality. the
majesty of believing at last
in everything that ever

was. the wonder of being
completely content
w/yourself & now.
the satisfaction of crossword
puzzles, runways, no snack
because 10,000 feet is
as high as we shall go
even though i feel as if
i am in the clouds holding
hands w/some angels
who have been waiting to
watch over me for all of
my natural life.

distant lover #2

dear marvin.
come see about me.
long way from home.
cold out here. no palm trees.
citrus fruit.
no 80-degree days
or beaches made of

sand.
& the
stores are out of
space heaters. my winter
soup is just a recipe
written on note cards. alarm rings
in the morning i do not move.
robert hayden needs to wake
his father from his
slumber.
lumber is
needed though
it ain't

sunday.
·come see about me, marvin.
did i tell you i'm lonely?
my mother came here
once. it was may & still
cold. she isn't afraid of anything
but the chill crawled up her
spine like snakes scarfing for
food. my mother always
been afraid of snakes.

can't blame this on harvey
fuqua. can't blame this on
berry gordy. can't blame this
on my awful singing voice. if only
i could sing, i might feel warmer.
buy me a hip home on outer drive
in detroit, get a fire started &
invite some singing football players

over to make a classic.
come see about me, marvin.
take me to your old haunts.
take me to l.a. or hawaii
hurry, i'm in trouble, man
i am one of the sensitive
people, need to be wanted
didn't you hear? my lady left
me out here in the cold like
a deer lost near an interstate.
please come show me the way
home. i'm pretty sure i don't
know how to get there anymore.

ontario, may 2012 (for elanna)

> *When I talk to people here, the first thing they sense
> is about [my] Americanness. That's the mask I have
> on for them. It's an incredible experience.*
> —Ta-Nehisi Coates (2015)

when we cross the border & are welcomed
we exhale. not like some terry mcmillan
novel but large liberating gusts. oxygen
flowing like a brisk body of water. our
minds clear as unused attics. we, on our
way to places never seen, un-concerned
w/where we shall wind up. no matter
what, it is not where we were born.
we will eat & sleep somewhere else tonight
& we will smile w/out shame better than ever.
we are baldwin or simone, ollie harrington per-
haps, as if we are back in the womb unaware
of the anger swirling around all of the time,
mosquitos in july. tornado clouds just off in
the distance taking form.

michigan haiku #2 (for j.d. porter)

january blizzard
the streets peppered
w/rock salt

red rooster bar, idlewild, michigan (for jeff & tamm)

of course there is a
jukebox that plays
mostly motown. every-

thing on the menu is
fried. people
are mostly happy.

they own this. they
ride golf carts through
the streets w/speakers

attached. they fire up
the barbecue. they drink
cold beer & ice tea.

they play scrabble &
try to fish & don't
have to worry "'bout a

thing." it is as if they
are finally free. like that
martin luther king jr.

speech. like derrick
bell's afrolantica.
like they left america.

like they never came
to america. like they
never worked the lines.

like they never helped
the unions get what
they got. like they

never had to sue to
become citizens. like
they never left arkansas

mississippi, alabama,
louisiana. like their
kids never did get shot

& killed in the motor
city. like they never rioted.
like they never rioted.

like they never got left
behind like they are
carcasses for buzzards.

like they got up this
morning & drove
to idlewild. they

came in this bar &
ordered fried catfish
& an ice-cold beer.

they put some coins in
the old jukebox.
they sat down &

ate their food slowly
& heard it again.
martin luther king jr.

talking crazy. like his
last name garvey. like
he really don't like it

here either. wants to
come home. right here,
where everyone loves

hot grease.

winter

cold michigan streets

"black lives matter" sign
nearly covered w/snow.

nowhere to hide

distant lover #3

mural of marvin eating mumbo sauce.
churches falling apart jesus on the cross.

broke streets w/stumble bums waving at buses.
people on board shouting 'bout lack of justice.

& my mom's back home making salmon cakes
kids these days no longer carry rakes
movies i see take too many takes
my mom's back home making salmon cakes

i work now up by the great lakes.
few up there are really fakes;
for goodness sakes
the city where i was formed
relies on these lies, skies
& french fries. pies & those
much-needed highs. we baked the
good in the city made of chocolate
that was always darker not lighter & so much
whiter. just ralph ellison again not visible.
invisible, not worried about being divisible.
back where it began, hidden slave marts
public schools full of someone else's arts.

so we created our own. roto toms backing up
like computer networks. they still rock beats
donning permanent smirks.

murals of marvin eating mumbo sauce. churches
falling apart, jesus on the cross.

broke streets w/stumble bums waving at buses.
people on board shouting 'bout lack of justice.

& my mom's back home making salmon cakes . . .

grand rapids (for k.k.)

then the snow came. like in that book
into thin air & i was happy we weren't
climbing the himalayas. i was just on my
way to grand rapids to do a seminar
on discrimination &
we were just about there when
someone tossed a white bed
sheet on our windshield &
our tires became skates on a
sheet of ice. now i knew
why much of the time on
these trips you could look
to the right or left & you
could see cars in the trees
driver out, air bags engaged,
cell phone in their ear.

but my driver is part of this.
she isn't from michigan
but her blood is thick too.
indiana. fort wayne. & it is
probably the same there she
says. she, as calm as
philippe petit on the wire between the
towers. she, a chef in a busy diner w/
one broken stove. she, a teller in
a crowded bank full of weekend check
cashers, computers down.

we will make it to the spot. show
our power point. i will speak because i
am george bailey; she is clarence diving in
the water. we could have been in the

trees, freezing & waiting for a tow w/
cell phones low on battery. instead,
i am like freddie hubbard following
hancock. my trumpet riffing redlining
blockbusting & acts that aren't fair
anywhere i can think of in any part of
the world.

this is my road. throw a white
sheet over the computer & i still
can play the melody. i am brian boitano or
scott hamilton sliding easy across the carpet
of a conference room at some old raggedy hotel.
but don't ask me to ever drive alone through
these roads. i leave those miracles to the locals.

o canada

he cuts my grass   detests the black president
this is the first thing he shares   then
says he's from canada   where gretzky was born
you know gretzky?   he & i have been in michigan

for the same amount of time   lost a parent   broke a heart
had ours broken   he is curious that i teach law &
know a few things   shouldn't i be mowing lawns
or laying cement?   a black man like me in a suit
more scarce in these parts than crawfish

i don't tell him i have seen him dancing butterball
naked on social media   i treat him w/respect   this mollifies
him though it is simple: ten toes ten fingers   nose   mouth   pain
        hearts
pumping blood   loves   but he still speaks always
unkindly of the black president   assumes i will get angry
like a child denied a toy   but i don't

his wife is dying   my big bro's wife has the same disease
this is where we all meet most days   it is our balm
& burden   we compare stories   when i see him
i just remain quiet   nod my head   he
invites me to church   i don't go   though my imagination surges:
people holding snakes   the most segregated hour in America
it's been called

last time i see him he's happy   his wife is alive but they
have split up   he doesn't cut lawns   he's wearing a suit
i attended a church last week   not his   i'm the only color
in the room but there are no snakes   i stand & sing
hymns   pray   feel like i am on pluto watching a hockey game
but no one there says anything bad about the black president
& there's a sign seen on their lawn: BLACK LIVES MATTER.

chicago (for haki)

goin' to chicago
by train plane or car

i say goin' to chicago
by train plane or car

seems like we been
driving forever

ain't get very far

chicago got some people
who love the lakefront gust

i say chicago got some people
who love the lakefront gust

only wear their mittens if
they mommas say they must

sweet home chicago
south side love me good

serve me fried chicken
like lightfoot said you would . . .

                but mostly
because haki has turned 70 &
we will be there to tell him it means
something. because
richard wright lived & worked
here on his way to brooklyn where
bigger would be born.

because one daughter wants to dance
another likes the egg on the michigan
mile & still another adores chicago style
popcorn & "dat donut" on state street.

because brother q works here & he speaks
to us like we also from oklahoma.

because krista & kelly & toni & so
many people are here & they are
not shooting anyone & they are
like a jacob lawrence painting:
triumphant.

because my lover used to live here
as a little girl & the city makes
her
eyes
sparkle
like
moonlit
oceans.

& if
her eyes
sparkle
my brain
swims
in a pool
of
dark
chocolate.

because she & i
stroll proudly
on the south side
& hold hands

& talk about
the first time we
saw *cooley high*.

because we can
cruise down
cottage grove &
west 77th street
& she shows me
where she once
skipped rope.

because st. sabinas
church is where
she got saved &
the priest who was
there for her is not
afraid of black people.

because her father saw
ernie banks hit a home
run once.

because somebody loved my
poetry in chicago like it was
dirty rice during a holiday meal
& so they let people eat a lot of it.

because here they take a good
look at my face. their lips
move softly. words come
out like songs from the motor city.
like a mother assuring her babies
the moon is not fake. the sun
is shining. the rain comes down
to cleanse the world. the march
of the good will always beat the

bad. the ever-present rhythm
of tied together time.

sweet home chicago

please just love me good

fry me some chicken
like gwen brooks said you would.

"reach out,"—*cooley high*, version, final scene
(for levi stubbs & the four tops)

song come on i
see preach running.
cochise's gon' home.
hard to understand it
when it came into
my space way back
when. barely here.
return from night
camp in the virginia
bush. sink into
seats at the town
theater new york avenue
motown movie.
my brother.
cousin.
things easy for boys
not yet army age
summertime & life is . . .

chill bumps. when
i hear the song now
levi & dem almost
makes me cry for
cochise even though
he ain't even real. he
somebody's screenplay.
but he still lives & breathes
& sings. he's fried
fish & kool-aid.
chocolate eclairs from
the good humor truck
in summer. flesh & bones

like todd gwynn '79
len bias '86
geo powell '93.
mistakes people say.
somebody pulled the wrong
lever. called the wrong person
home way too soon.

preach is reading his poem.
it is dreadful but full of love.
he balls it up tosses it to forever.
takes off running fast to-
wards his life like
he chasing someone
who just stole his bike.
he seeking some shelter
comfort
new energy
as the song
soars.

i understand now.
we go on.
we are built like that.
even though we feel like
we can't comprehend
the confusion. when
all hope is gone.

portrait of black woman, exit 64, toledo, w/beautiful afro

i pass by here for just a few seconds & i want
her booth. i will wait longer to pay her

my toll money. i don't mind sharing her w/
others who pass this way like me. they don't

love her like i do anyway. i love her more than
belafonte's voice, ellington's blazers, billie

holiday's gardenia. i take my trips back east
knowing i shall see her when i return. we

will exchange brief glances, smiles, stare into
each other's eyes: mother to son, son to mother.

see across the centuries. she knows who i am;
i know who she is. perhaps her people once

worked on one of the lines. or maybe she is here
because she once toiled somewhere that is also

gone because the lines are gone. yet, she always
smiles & sustains me as i press on through

what i have accepted like the postman delivering
the mail in a blizzard. up north where it is

bitterly cold for much too long. isolated & forgotten
to everyone. but still, i do not get an e-z pass.

if i had an e-z pass i would just zip through the gates
in seconds. some system taking note of me,

isolation even more obvious. like dead animals
always on the roads because no one comes to pick

them up quickly in this empty space. but, of course,
her afro draws me here. the last gasp of what was.

we, of cotton gins, hot factories, automated tellers, express
checkouts in retail. our glance puts that on hold but

not for long. it is a question to which we have no answers.
we zombies w/our smartphones & impatience. &

did i tell you the other day i saw a car on the road w/
no driver. it never moved too fast, always cut on the

blinker to change lanes & this is what we have
decided to do to all the women w/beautiful afros.

never will they be there to smile one day. no one to help us
to understand what means the most in this frozen unforgiving air.

those small moments that last a lifetime. & when they are
gone, there will be nothing else out here but the cold.

kalamazoo boogie

give me a word that rhymes w/voodoo
my children shout loud: kalamazoo

teju cole born in kalamazoo
putting down words holler hoodoo

there is a city here named for saint lou
far up north, from kalamazoo

a bunch of poets in kalamazoo
are always sure their verse rings true

haiku tanka sonnet & stew
ghazal elegy kalamazoo

took a trip down to kalamazoo
in search of jesus, in search of you

no one knows i haven't a clue
the origin of the word: kalamazoo

indigenous inhabitants of kalamazoo
they got their own ways, got their own hue

the running joke now timbuktu
if you don't where—kalamazoo

highway 1-3-1 kalamazoo
in '74 they closed the city zoo

sold the bookmobile in 2-0-1-2
but people love poetry in kalamazoo

bonnie jo campbell lives in kalamazoo
american salvage totally true

yankee named jeter lived here too
boy learned to ball in kalamazoo

met a judge born in kalamazoo
loves his mom, she was born there too

inside his courtroom, i think of the zoo
men in shackles from kalamazoo

if only they had listened down in kalamazoo
now they gotta do what they tell them to do

remember the guy who picked up a shoe
tried to clock the prez, some desert snafu

wasn't kalamazoo, that rhymes w/gazoo
yahoo yahoo this poem sniffs glue

shout out a city that rhymes w/shampoo
once i ate some coneys in kalamazoo

the negro in minneapolis
(for prince & philando castile)

that time i drove to minneapolis from
east lansing to read stories w/some black
people & ate nicoise salads
saw dozens of somalians who
stood outside in the cold &
kicked a soccer ball all day &
smoked cheap american cigarettes
that clouded their spaces like in card
games or bowling alleys in the old
days when life was simple   AM radio
black & white television   hot
dogs boiled & eaten w/mustard
george mikan shooting hook shots
for the lakers

the city recalled that time or maybe it
was st paul   the other
of the twins   where f scott
learned how to gatsby but also
why he had to leave & go in search
of his soul   or maybe it was a
black woman poet who loved to dance
as if dancing was writing haiku   & so
she threw a party for a prince who lived in
the city   the same prince who zoomed
to life not long after the days of boiled
hot dogs w/mustard   AM radio was dying
& people smoked cheap cigarettes in
bowling alleys

missed that party but so many came to write haiku
that evening   no one had space to write anything

they just danced & clapped their hands & partied
like it was the end of days   somalians ruled my
evening instead   something about men darker than
chunks of coal kicking around a soccer ball w/not
a care in the world in one of the coldest places is
reassuring   like on airplane flights & they
begin serving mixed drinks at 38,000 feet

only other thing i did in minneapolis besides poems & stories
& somalians is jog in the snow   flurries floated around
me like confetti   like when mikan's lakers won it all & they
were champagne-drinking happy   it was a wondrous time
did not even know then that dred scott once lived here as a
slave long before roger taney declared him nothing   but
lester young blew horn on the north side here in the '20s in
        his father's
band & gordon parks played blues piano in some brothel downtown
before he made magic w/those cameras

& the prince of this city who zoomed to life was still alive dreaming
& writing songs & throwing parties that lasted forever   philando
castile had not yet reached for his wallet & then all those cameras
& marchers & tweeters came running to talk about it like joe
kapp running for a first down across an ice rink of a football field to
try again to win it all for the locals

view from paul laurence dunbar home, dayton, ohio

like a snap
chat clip it
all comes back:

my best friend ronnie
beavers, gone
from this world
now, is reading
"negro love song."
he is like a minister
on sunday.
this is third grade
lasalle elementary.
we both
have chosen
poems to recite
written somewhere
on these empty streets
once vibrant & full
of confident souls
not living in kentucky
somewhere laughing
on this side of the
river ohio

ronnie & i stood up
shaking our papers
yelled out
verse like we are
selling used cars
at auctions
neither of us yet

understood
masks caged
birds   mostly
young   nervous
full of cold milk
graham cracker
history laughter rises
later in our bellies
negro love songs
that don't grin or
lie   for our wonderful
verse we receive
the ultimate reward:

we get to shake the erasers
clean of the day's chalk
at the end of the school day.
& we banged them together
that day w/a new, joyous
rhythm:

"jump back
honey
jump back

jump back
honey
jump back

jump back
honey
jump back . . ."

denny mcclain, in garden city, michigan
(for scott & dan)

as we wait for court to begin in garden city
michigan   we grab lunch at a coney joint   when i
moved here i was in the dark about coneys   to me
a coney was that amusement park city in new york

where the movie *the warriors* ends w/that stupid
gangbanger clicking beer bottles & chanting for the
warriors to come outside   i thought coneys were
something i had never had before like monkey brains or

steak tartare   but a coney is a hot dog & the one
on my plate in garden city recalls attending baseball games
as a kid at rfk stadium in washington d.c.   i am rooting for the
senators & we are the worst team in the league even though

we now have the great denny mcclain pitching for us   denny
once a star for the tigers won 31 in '68 but then gambled his
way out of detroit to washington d.c. & loserville   walter
johnson would be ashamed of this   even the great ted williams

our manager can't make this mayhem a miracle   but truth is we
        didn't
need denny   we are catastrophe   even worse   we gave the tigers
two of my favorite players of all time for denny: aurelio rodriguez
        & ed
brinkman   ed is a vacuum at shortstop & he chokes up on

his bat just like me when i played little league   & aurelio is gold
at third base for so many years but then was killed in some crazy car
accident in downtown detroit many years after he retired   i don't
        eat
the coney   i order a greek salad to go   my coney sits

40

on my plate like a beautiful woman i once loved but will never
     hold in
my arms again   concys make me think of denny
ed & aurelio & that one day the senators moved away from
washington to texas & were bought by some stupid oilman

who one day would become president & start a terrible war   i
     want to
forget about that too but here there are so many coney joints
i just focus on the good times: ed at short   aurelio is at third & i
am in the stands w/a hot dog & i don't know a thing about denny
     mcclain.

the lansing negro

invisible
& visible

no
work in

any
paint factory

playing
around w/

colors.
no college

either.
& at

first
no eye

contact.
cyborg like.

want
to be

left
alone. ellison's

man
w/out a

name.
eat a

yam
off a

truck
in the

north.
disappear, won't

fight
anyone in

a
cigar-filled

arena,
steal electricity

eventually
they arrive

at
my door

we
realize again

the
barber shop

cuts
afros, fades

sells
hot items

hums
w/its

own
linguistic love.

salons
braid hair

trade
rumors like

cards
in fish

the
churches shout

loud
sing "total

praise"
as good

as
smallwood. we

all
got here

same
bad voyage.

a
doubt-driven

distance
between us

gone
now. my

how
they can

relate
laugh, share

their
unfamiliar journeys

of
strange circles

cold
rooms, meetings.

we
will speak

to
one another

in
public now

always
as if

we
go back

many
generations. we

want
to be

seen
by those

who
matter &

who
know how

it
feels to

be
unnoticeably human.

ingham county

two-lane
roads.

black tar.
mailboxes.

white lines.
pass signs.

do not pass.
fields shaved

like face.
stalk as beard.

barren acres
like razor

stubble ready
to rise

again next
season. not

pretty this
evening

morning, any-
time, yet

pampered
waiting on

hands, ma-
chine, water.

life again.
beauty off

this hidden
speedway.

shortcut
of folklore.

freedom
& life of

way. where
they don't

bother to
plow. you

folks are
on your

own just
like you

want it
to be.

like, imagine
eddie albert

in *green acres*
saying

fresh air as
the show

comes on. but
they got

mobile phones
out here

facebook,
gmail. some

even have
instagram.

3

no ordinary pain

distant lover #4 (for leon ware)

dear lover.

marvin & i still most nights
& the incessant sound of space
heater. on the floor beside my
bed: scattered books.
i phone doing pandora
i want you.
it was not supposed
to be like this. but i never could
sing very well. & no one comes
to visit anymore. especially since
the polar vortex. that is the year
i thought i wanted to die. instead
i made jerk cod stew each night
& waited for the messiah on the couch
alone. our children slept like squirrels do
each winter. you still nowhere
to be seen. the music got me through
this end of the world. igloo inside an igloo.
& the space heater never stopped humming.
& the woman next door had a snow blower.
took me three weeks to dig my car out of the ice.
the arctic in my backyard. siberia said
hello. i learn the lyrics to "sexual
healing" in reverse. if only you had come
& sat next to me on the couch things might
have been less lonely. i would not be writing this
poem. & maybe this poem would be about
love.

inkster blues (for greg)

way down there in inkster weeds grows out of cement
i say way down there in inkster weeds grows out of cement
the people down there in inkster want to know where all
the money they had don' went.

down the way in inkster there is just one auto plant making cars
i say down the way in inkster there is just one auto plant making
        cars
a lot of churches & used car shops, too many overcrowded bars.

we rode 96 to inkster trying to save a woman's home.
i say we rode 96 to inkster trying to save a woman's home
the courthouse was so crowded, i thought of the fall of rome.

we rode through the streets of inkster in search of something to do
i say we rode through the streets of inkster in search of something
        to do
stopped off in some coney joint & spilled hot chili on my shoe

went to city hall in inkster & there was no one there in charge
i say went to city hall in inkster & there was no one there in charge
young man on the street tell me people here used to live large

so i took my leave of inkster i seen enough to write this song
i say so i took my leave of inkster seen enough to write this song
like all them other michigan cities somebody then don' her wrong

detroit sketch #1 (for m.l.)

looking closely i now see the chevys fords chryslers
lining these streets like paupers standing in soup lines.
years ago everyone really did still believe in this.
they bought the cars. they embraced history. they sacrificed.
they were devoted followers. not a cult but invested,
so they thought. learning love is not always reciprocal
& adam smith is not around to explain anything.
there are no invisible hands seen around here anymore
that is except for hands that once pulled levers.

in detroit my korean import does not get keyed.
this is the dead folklore; david halberstam writer prophetic.
as i look again at these chevys fords chryslers
lining these streets like paupers standing in soup lines
i finally make sense of this love gone bad
we are the 21st century; the epoch of wi-fi.
assembly lines are now full of phones, pads, robots
there are no invisible hands seen around here anymore
that is except for hands that once pulled levers.

the road to flint, michigan

like
feta
cheese
crumbled
for
greek
salad.

flint river blues

water's polluted
governor knows we not
'sposed to drink

water's polluted
governor knows we not
'sposed to drink

my kids wake up in the mornin'
say daddy i feel like i can't think

fat cats changed the water
to stuff their pockets w/loot

fat cats changed the water
to stuff their pockets w/loot

got nothin' to do w/people
we manure on the bottom of a boot

it's all 'bout the money, that's how's it
always been
it's all 'bout the money, that's how's it
always been

governor would let fifty die, if
he knew it would save him ten

we stood in line for water, in some
dead of winter days
stood in line for water, in
some dead of winter days

the way these people governin'
just call it their evil ways.

all the folks in power say they didn't know
we was drinkin' death
all the folks in power say they
didn't know we was drinkin' death

emails say they liars &
my name is not macbeth.

media finally showed up
exposed this crime to all
media finally showed up
exposed this crime to all

governor & all his bureaucrats
need to take a fall

gon' be a long time before this is over
i guess you've heard it on the news
gon' be a long time before this is over
i guess you've heard the news

& we will never let the world
forget about the flint river blues . . .

mason, michigan, housing court (evictions #1)

and the sheriff will be on his way . . .

it is as if all of us are bots being called
by someone wanting to alter their

phone service. all day long, hour after
hour like on the line in the ford motor

plants but even more synchronized. sini-
ster. everyone in their places. assemble

these hopeful arrangements in minutes. we all
know this is no way to live. like skating on a lake

before the winter freeze locks in hard, even
though your parents told you never to do that.

evictions #2

out here, a lawyer
for a landlord tells
me people he's trying
to kick out in the
dead of winter don't
deserve lawyers.

like i am a priest
speaking w/someone
on death row:

faith
mercy
jesus

someone walks in
suddenly
hits me over the
head w/a chair.

eviction #3 (a lawyer's solo)

she wants us to keep playing her song.
collectively we are the dexter gordon
band on that long endless version of
body & soul. the lp where dexter is
surrounded by smoke on the cover.
after he hung up "the horse," didn't
care about anything at all except
the sound of his band, tenor, cheers
claps in clubs in paris
denmark, away from
streets that stripped
him of himself.

i tell her i am not dexter.
& even if i was, this is not
europe &
we are not
in the moment
gathering that something
from the cosmos that
saves you from yourself.
she doesn't understand.
even when they tell us
stop playing
pack up your horns
the show's over because
we're tired of that tune
heard it far too many times now.
makes us feel downright irresponsible
sometimes. like we have mistakenly
given opium to a bunch of children.

eviction #4 (lansing court)

crab claws.

everywhere.

nonstop
snapping.

living for the city (for stevie wonder)

at the lansing school for the blind
the boarded-up buildings do the talking.
people here living just enough like a boy
named steveland from saginaw who arrived here
half famous. mouth organ near his fingertips, singing
christmas songs way before this became the
frontline. pastime paradise. ted hull w/his
own terrible sight showing the boy how to walk
straight lines that he will need when he makes
music down in the motor city. don't want to
bore you w/the morning sun. because lately
these streets aren't happy or lovely. no one is calling
to say they love anything either. this is in need of
love today. the parks. storefront churches w/
barely any members. houses welcoming squatters
& rats. there is no joy inside tears. everyone around
here would move to saturn if they could. be there always.
this no ordinary pain, no ordinary pain. knocking many
off of their feet in this village ghetto land that
hasn't done nothing in a very long time.

children of the reagan democrats

medical marijuana on michigan avenue
amidst fava bean & fatoosh, eminem
imitators & many meth labs . . .

> imma skinny white kid.
> twenty-ish. got more tattoos than
> a star athlete. crewcut, black sweat
> pants, hoodie. always high on
> somethin' & not tryin' to obey anyone.
> still, i won't get shot by the police.
> even if i'm holdin' steel. even if i make
> a "furtive gesture" like my lawyer say
> once. i reek of smokes, cheap cologne
> i jacked from the mall, all-nighters in
> county lock-up. but still i won't get shot
> by the police. i don't take baths or showers.
> imma threat to myself & whoever
> might be around on one of my
> bad trips into outer space on some
> haze, shrooms, or something called
> double dip blue star, but i won't get shot
> by the police. this i know. like some people
> know their souls are saved & that people
> die in threes . . .

medical marijuana on michigan avenue
amidst fava bean & fatoosh, eminem
imitators & many meth labs . . .

> i'm originally from dallas.
> the most dangerous street in the
> country was my block people say.
> folk don't know. say i'm

just hype, some flava flav shit.
just because imma white dude.
think i ain't got no street cred.
they say i'm fishing rod, clam
snout, smack my lady after a
shout. ate too much shrimp got
premature gout. say i think i
can fight but ain't never had a
bout. but here i am & that's
w/out a doubt. all of it is true.
i try to do right. but this me.
i can't do right. tell me to show
up at noon. i show late.
tell me to not use dope & piss
clean imma get high that night.
& tell me i ain't who i am &
i can show you where i'm from.
talk is cheap anyway. like soap from
the dollar store. try me, i will take you
to where i've been. you know where to
find me otherwise. out here w/
a bunch of devils . . .

medical marijuana on michigan avenue
amidst fava bean & fatoosh, eminem
imitators & many meth labs.

black hawk is down!
black hawk is down!
i sleep w/my gun. if
i sleep. i am like an owl in
a tree at night. or day. i can't
get it out my head. like the
first time you get carsick
or the first casket you stare
into & the person there is
someone you knew well &

talked to more than once. but
imagine even closer than that.
this is hard. like calculus that i
never passed even when i was
pulling all-nighters. why am i here
again? i will never be normal.
you set a house on fire & it
burns. you can rebuild it
but it is not the same house. it
is like a man who can't imagine tomorrow,
a boy who can't do math no matter how
much he tries. i am the black
hawk that's down. i wish i heard
voices at night or anytime. i hear
nothing. i just lie awake & remember
all of it like it is still happening
again & my gun is out of bullets.

at malcolm x street, lansing, michigan
(for earl little*)

& just around the corner is where they killed
your father. the streetcar tracks long
gone. bus service jettisoned them back in the
'50s. parking lot marks the intersection. bus
drivers sit there now & then & surf their
smartphones more than their customers. there is
nothing marking the death of this man, a garveyite,
dead right here regardless. nothing of his pride,
unbitten tongue, audacious nerve. if he had not come
as he came perhaps you would not have come as you
had come. if he had not spoken loud maybe you would
have been meek & things might still be as they
were so long ago & for so long. he never danced
so others could feel big. he died a hundred
deaths for what he believed. he rode his wagon
into the most difficult of places. sundown towns like
owosso where he chose to risk his demise rather than become the
walking dead. still we will never know what really
happened out here at this crossroad that is as quiet
as a city park mid-morning every day. did you tell
haley what you believed or what you knew? was it
real or just soapbox chatter to hide your wounded heart?
but this we do know: he walked upright. he spoke like
the earth beneath his feet was his as well. instead of
dismissing him maybe we can seek to understand his
time. he, a man of humbled strength & infinite love. he,
a man who cared for the world. he, a man who did not
die in vain. unacknowledged, yet still adored in this silence.

* Earl Little was the father of the African American revolutionary spokesman Malcolm
X. Little, according to various accounts, was murdered by white supremacists in the
city of Lansing on September 28, 1931.

distant lover #5

dear lover.

like
scott kelly

astronaut.

300-plus
days.

outer space
every night.

grand rapids, civil war reenactment

at last: abe lincoln.
black broadcloth
coat, sugarloaf
top hat & the beard,
a piece of costume
of course, but yet,
something essential
to the man must be worn,
grace bedell's wishes
in a letter a piece of
history we can never
not mention now.

there were only bluecoats
around him; there being
no ambivalence or longing
for some other ending like
historical fragments that
are part of life back east.
like who knew? across the
potomac river from the
great city, arlington ceme-
tery once robert e.
lee's family home. &
maryland? frederick
douglass & harriet
tubman ran away from
that place. not to mention
those annual war re-
enactments, those
godless displays
of our lowest mo-
ments: confede-

rate flags, south
trying to rise like a
vamp from their own
dirt. abe nowhere to
be seen amongst
fake cannon
smoke & "charge."
antietam. manassas.
gettysburg. but
this is the north. union.
& no, not UAW
but the blue. God &
country folks. 90,000
here would put
their bodies on the
line. nearly 15,000 would
die. they mean it.
death for their demo-
cracy, for what they
conceived, northwest
ordinance their constitu-
tion. no africans in chains
sold on blocks like antique
furniture. this (for some)
is the other door of
no return. there it is
the detroit river;
many shall vanish in the
night. reappear in
morning in cities
beyond this republic.
dresden. lakeshore.
windsor. the brits
aren't saintly but
they were done w/
the business of flesh.
we will shoot each

other over it religiously
for a bit longer.
got a bullet especially
for this tall guy
strolling through down-
town grand rapids. do
all the people
gawking know
he never ever came
here once during
the war? maybe we
really are all
staring at a ghost?

confederate flag, michigan #1

north wind blows wildly.
two boys come out. take
it down. fold it careful &
slow, like at a funeral.

ann arbor (alpha poem)

The instruction in standard English of children who use "black English" at home by insensitive teachers who treat the children's language system as inferior can cause a barrier to learning to read and use standard English.
—Judge Charles W. Joiner, *Martin Luther King Jr. Elementary School v. Ann Arbor School District*
473 F. Supp 1371 (1979)

ann arbor
black & blue
city of sensitive souls
do you understand
ebonics?
from your
ghettos
have
i seen a
jaded
kind of
lost brother.
marred.
negated.
our
people
quietly dying
resigned to fate
saying
they are
under the yoke.
voided, this
way of life
xeroxed
year after year, in this
zoo.

(alternate take)

ann arbor. you
be trippin'
cuz; you
don't
ever
feel really
giddy 'bout us.
hate?
i don't
just wanna be
kissed
liberally;
malcolm x
negro
obsolete
passé
quickly
returned
some
to
underground railroad.
vanish like bootsy.
walk like "the time."
x klan
you ever hear that song:
"zoom zoom," want to fly away, huh?

when i see the exit sign for cleveland on the ohio turnpike now (alpha poem)

1.
absent at school.
boy.
christmas.
did he move?
every day the internet.
fake
gun
hypothesis?
i
just . . .
kick me in the mouth.
lye water in my face.
malevolent.
no!
oh
please.
quell the
reasoning.
so
tamir was
up to something?
veto!
we know
xenophobia would.
yell something.
zip it.

2.
& his sister was right there
beside him.
care for him at the end or not.

dear tamir.
everyone loves you.
feel my hand.
god loves you.
hold on.
i am here.
just hold on now.
keep holding on.
let us say what is.
man is man.
n-words are wretched.
or maybe devo. the
police are
quiet.
routine.
so we
take a breath.
understand.
vow to not
waste your
x-it.
you are twelve.
zebras live longer than that.

yellow school bus

he rose from his seat
he's nine   he understands

it all already
or at least
he thinks he does

he begins the chant
a familiar cadence

"white power white
power"   he raises

his fist   he turns to
my child   like a wino

turns towards the
liquor store   gamblers

towards race tracks   he
says what he says

his mother   father   cousins
uncles' history   the school

the one where the bus
is headed   the one w/

the civil war exhibit
confederate flags   no

explanation of the thing
he will get called out

for this   the bus driver
tells him so   this is the

north   2011 not 1911   everyone on the

bus chuckles at him   he will hear
more later perhaps at home

he sort of gets it   he has
been told over & over
to smoke but not smoke

his parents coughing   clutch-
ing kools or camels   dragging

on them slow & beautifully
as he learns how to raise

his fist & chant   but oh how he
hates the smell of cigarette

smoke especially in a car
w/the windows rolled

up   moon in the sky
north wind touching his

face delicately like the
dark silence of night

confederate flag #2

one of those license
tags on the front of
a pickup truck.

rusted,

bent & cracked

faded in color

nearly falling
off.

let your love come shining through

distant lover #6

dear lover. i sleep the other way now.
my head at the foot of the bed. my feet
at the headboard. it is the only way
to make sense of now. think of it like this:

> i am a golfer. i start by taking the ball
> out of the cup & putting it away from the green.
> & then i hit it again, w/an iron. soon i will be
> back at the tee.

i don't sleep well at night. i tell people
you are just away working & they
don't believe it. they snicker when
they leave the room.
it does sound outlandish.
like a guy i knew growing
up used to say his father
was in a witness protection
program whenever we asked
"where's your father?"
eventually he lost his mind
& went on a crime spree
because he was tired of
explaining why his father
did not tell him he loves him.
he spent many years in prison.
he sent me a facebook message
recently. "hello," he said, "how
are you? heard you are having
problems. let me tell you:
i sleep the other way in bed. my head
where my feet belong. my
feet at the headboard. it is the only

way to make sense of this. it is
the only way to stop myself from
going back to prison."

small town folklore

says he rides to court
on a horse. & i don't mean
a motorcycle. saddle & all
no rifle strapped to his back
no cigar in his mouth but he
rocks cowboy boots w/the
best.

if michigan had the death
penalty he would have
sent more than a few
to the gallows.

all women he encounters no
matter how old are called by
their first name.

remember those old western
films where the judge ran the whole
territory?

yet, when i sit down in
front of him, it feels like i am
suddenly on a sun porch, ice-
cold lemonade, banana bread
just out the oven, some hospitality
to speak of above the mason dixon.
i am somebody for a moment
not some museum piece. i am more
than blue blazer, gray slacks,
fake oxford tie; i am part of the ameri-
can epic. a tale of effort & endurance
that makes some hearts skip.

men place their hands there when
francis scott key's best gets looped
again. if i was not here, standing, sitting,
showing some it was all worth the fight
things might fall apart again like the union,
1861.

he would have fought in that war, given
his life w/out regret like the millions.
he believes in all of it ten times more
than i ever can. & he believes that
my suit & tie & the legal papers
in my lap say i too would lay down my life
so others might live for this.

i got to be honest:
i do like sun porches
love banana bread
but all of it makes my
head hurt most days.
i do not even know who
i am really. my mother,
grandchild of share-
croppers. my father had
to ride on the back of the
bus when he was in the army.
if i remind him of this
he just says i need to
live in the here & now.

but i am in the here & now. in his
territory. where people say he rides a
horse to work & everyone laughs at all
of his jokes. he calls all women by
their first names & no one ever says
anything. & the war has not been won
no matter what he might believe. this

is his house. i am just a visitor. when i
exit the doors i will ride fast on my horse
back to some place that will never feel
like home.

guns, bats & books

Every person has a right to bear arms for the defense
of himself and the state.

(Michigan Constitution)

there is a bat in my house.
everyone thinks this is normal.

when i call places that eradicate
bats from houses they say they

really don't do that. they tell me
open up the doors, windows,

wait for it to fly out. it makes no
sense. sort of like all the guns

some people have here. more guns
than toothbrushes combs & bottles

of cheap cologne that couldn't get rudy
valentino a date. guns loved more than

jelly beans at easter. one guy loved guns
so much he rolled into the public library

rifle strapped to his back & was turned
away. broke his heart. he might as well

have been some black person in georgia in
1930 trying to rent a room for the night. he

sued. & won. you got a right to carry rifles
in the public library now but you can't eat food

in there. they should open a gun shop down-
stairs where they sell used books. they should

close down the computer room & teach gun
safety. they should sell ammo & not used books

to raise money for library upkeep. they should
arrest anyone carrying books concealed under

their coats. they should make the librarians teach
us how to load. they should turn the whole thing
into a 24-hour gun range.

there is a bat in my house & i do not know how to get
        it out. it flew around, landed on some ledge &
is now just lying there like count dracula waiting
        for the sun to set. i can't take any chances. i plan
to buy a gun. i am going to shoot it down right away.
        if you don't act fast bats will think that they can
stay in your house forever. i read that in some book.

robert hayden, university of michigan campus
(a skinny—for truth thomas)

imagine his stroll today to
poetry
class.
briefcase.
eyeglasses.
poetry.
smartphones.
tweets.
snaps.
poetry.
to imagine his stroll today!

distant lover #7

dear marvin.

i am reading thich nhat hanh's *how to love.* because I have failed at
    love again. just like
i have always failed science courses in school. especially chemistry.
    this explains why i
sleep alone night after night. this must be some government-
    funded science experiment.
like i am all alone in some petri dish being stared at by people in
    lab coats, mouths covered, gloves on to protect them from
    something that might make them feel awfully lonely all of a
    sudden. i would like to see what they have written in their
    notebooks when they leave the room & talk. perhaps it will
    make my lover return sooner or visit more often. lie here in
    bed w/me in this cold, dark place, listening to some of your
    most beautiful songs, & feeling loved again, at last . . .

Acknowledgments

The writer wishes to thank the following publications for publishing some of the poetry contained in this collection: "distant lover #1" and "yellow school bus" in *Forage*; "mardi gras in east lansing" in *Pudding Magazine*; "michigan haiku #2" in *Midnight Circus*; "winter" and "o canada" in *Sojourners Magazine*; "inkster blues" and "the road to flint, michigan" in the *Wayne Literary Review*; and "detroit sketch #1" in *Poetry Breakfast*.

In addition, thanks, as always, to my entire family (especially Elanna and the Girls and my mum), the ancestors, and my ever-present DC poetry family global. To the Kimbilio crew (thanks to the Black storytellers); to Annie, and everyone at Wayne State University Press; and to the following individuals who read or supported some or all of this work, as it evolved: Randall Horton, Linette Allen, Heather Buchanan, the MSU Center for Poetry, and Jeff and Tamm Wray. Finally, thanks to Joan Howarth (Dean); to everyone at MSU & the College of Law; and lastly, the truly "good" people of Michigan and the American Midwest, for their spirit, character, and perseverance.

About the Author

 brian g. gilmore, born and raised in Washington, D.C., is author of three previous collections of poetry, including *We Didn't Know Any Gangsters*, a 2014 NAACP Image Award nominee and 2015 Hurston-Wright Award nominee. He is a recipient of the 2001 and 2003 Individual Artist Award from the MidAtlantic Arts Council and was nominated in 1997 for the Larry Neal Writers Award, in the essay category. He served as writer in residence at St. Mary's College in April 2016 and poet in residence at Duke Ellington School for the Arts in June 2016. He has published writings in a wide array of genres, including fiction, essays, book reviews, and academic writings on topics related to race, housing, and inequality. He has been a columnist with the Progressive Media Project since 2002, taught writing at Catholic University of America, and was a member of the D.C. WritersCorps community writing workshop program from 1995 to 1997. His writings have most recently appeared in *Counterpunch*, *The Sun Magazine*, *Sojourners*, and *The New York Times*. He is on the board of the D.C. Creative Writing Workshop, in Washington D.C. He teaches social justice law at Michigan State University.